Grammar

Section 1 — Word Types

Page 2 — Nouns

1. You should have underlined: **zoo, lions, monkeys, Ella, animals**.
   You should have circled: **excitement, childhood, courage**.

2. Any suitable nouns. Examples:
   Everyone feels so much **happiness** about doing more drawings of **cats**.
   The **team** of **cyclists** moves really slowly along the **road**.
   A group of **humans** could be called a **crowd**.

Page 3 — Adjectives

1. You should have underlined: **cold, dark, howling, leafless, torrential, little, jittery, creaking, tired, old**.

2. Any suitable adjectives.
   Examples:
   The **golden** sun shone brightly over the **green** valley and the **hungry** cows stood munching the **long** grass.

3. Any suitable sentence.
   Example:
   The silly, bossy boy made a nasty comment.

Page 4 — Verbs

1. Laurie often **goes** to the shop and **buys** some bread.
   Our house **has** a garage and **is** really big.
   We always **visit** Habeeb at the weekend and **take** him out.
   He always **does** the washing and **cleans** the windows.
   The cows **eat** the grass and **watch** the walkers go by.

2. Any suitable sentences.
   Examples:
   The butler serves Lord Lazyton his morning coffee.
   The mole claps whenever he sees the sun.
   Ruth's pony smiles all day long.
   Dylan cries when his TV breaks.

Page 5 — Adverbs

1. Any suitable adverbs.
   Examples:
   Jarome **suddenly** decided to book a holiday to Wales.
   The girls **secretively** passed a note to the boys.
   Mum and Dad are **really** pleased with me.
   The test was **extremely** difficult.
   I will **definitely** tell Katie the truth tomorrow.
   The teacher shouted **loudly** at the class.

2. Any suitable sentence.
   Example:
   Jill was really surprised — Edward was probably going to win the race now.

Pages 6 to 8 — Synonyms and Antonyms

1. **front — back, big — small, hot — cold, dry — wet**

2. Marvin feels drowsy — he's just so **sleepy** today.
   They live in a huge house — it's simply **enormous**.
   The party was quite rowdy — people kept saying how **noisy** it was.

3.

4. Any suitable synonyms.
   Examples:
   untrue — **false**, brave — **courageous**, impolite — **rude**, yell — **shout**, elegant — **graceful**, irregular — **odd**

5. Across:
   1 **first**, 2 **happy**, 3 **early**, 4 **high**, 5 **wrong**
   Down:
   1 **fast**, 2 **hard**, 3 **take**, 4 **tiny**, 5 **rich**

6. She always exaggerates her achievements — she's so **arrogant**.
   I think Humphrey is a bit strange — his behaviour is very **curious**.
   There are few birds around here. In fact, their numbers are **sparse**.

7. Adjective: **simple**
   Any suitable synonyms and antonyms. Examples:
   Synonym: **easy**
   Antonym: **hard**
   Adverb: **quickly**
   Any suitable synonyms and antonyms. Examples:
   Synonym: **speedily**
   Antonym: **slowly**

8. Any suitable sentences.
   Examples:
   We are so **near** to the end now.
   I don't like it when my sisters **push** me.
   Louise is a **lovely** girl.
   Rebecca felt very **weak** after her operation.

Page 9 — Pronouns

1. My dog Rover hates going for walks along the path **which** runs by the canal. When **we** walk there, he barks a lot, especially when he sees Mr Mildew, **whose** Poodle then starts woofing back at us. After a while, Mrs Waterweed, **who** lives in a canal boat, always opens her window and shouts at **us**.

2. Carrie decided to do it <u>herself</u>.
   Some stories are fictional, <u>others</u> are based on real events.
   The dog scratched <u>itself</u> when nobody was looking.
   The children tasted all of the cakes but thought <u>theirs</u> were the best.

Grammar

Section 2 — Clauses and Phrases

Page 10 — Clauses

1. Main clauses: **We like pizza**, **I'm going out**
   Subordinate clauses: **while she watched the film**, **although I'm not sure**, **If we leave now**

2. Any suitable relative clauses.
   Examples:
   I looked at Caroline, **who seemed very angry**, and ran.
   Liam read the sign, **which was in French**, very slowly.
   We went to the shop, **which sells comics**, with Shaun.
   He met Sasha, **who moved here from Russia**, last year.

Page 11 — Phrases

1. You should have ticked: **a creepy goblin**, **very slowly**, **some pictures**, **these biscuits**, **on the top shelf**, **big birds of prey**.

2. You should have circled: **on the wall**, **to the zoo**, **at the back**.
   You should have underlined: **Jim plays golf**, **he knows Lucy**, **we hid from them**.

3. Any suitable phrases.
   Examples:
   on the ceiling
   a green lizard

Page 12 — Sentences

1. **Simple**:
   Professor Thinkalot is inventing a time machine.
   Paul went to Barcelona on Tuesday.
   Complex:
   Ruby went outside even though it was snowing.
   Kevin often sings when he's having a shower.
   Compound:
   I stood at the bus stop, and I waited for the bus.

2. Any suitable sentences.
   Examples:
   Simple: My favourite subject is German.
   Complex: We go to Wales when the weather is nice.
   Compound: I enjoy tennis, but I don't enjoy badminton.

Section 3 — Linking Ideas

Page 13 — Conjunctions

1. We're learning to grow fruits and vegetables **because** we have a new garden at school. Mr Beeman let us plant potatoes **even though** we haven't done it before, **and** Miss Everton says we can plant some carrots **as soon as** we have time, **so** we're getting the soil ready.

2. Example:
   We're building a house because we need more room.
   Dad says I can watch, but I have to be careful since it can be dangerous.

Page 14 — Linking Paragraphs with Adverbials

1. You should have underlined these phrases:
   I do chores <u>four times a week</u>. <u>Despite this</u>, my sister gets more pocket money than me. <u>Of course</u>, if her chores were harder it would be fair. <u>After all</u>, I do the same jobs as her, and I do them better. <u>For example</u>, I make sure I wash up properly. My sister, <u>on the other hand</u>, makes a mess of it!

2. There are many reasons why we need to have P.E. lessons in school.
   Firstly, it's important to keep healthy by doing regular exercise. It would be great for everyone to have the opportunity to keep fit.
   In addition, sport can be really good fun. There are lots of different things to try and there's something out there for everyone.
   Despite this, some people think that sport isn't as important as other subjects. They think P.E. lessons are waste of time.
   However, I think that we need a balanced school day both inside and outside the classroom.

Page 15 — Linking Paragraphs Using Repetition

1. You should have written these phrases:
   Living in London
   At the football

2. Any sentences which link to the previous paragraph and use a repeated word or phrase.
   Examples:
   Her grandson, Ben, didn't wear the jumper, even though she thought he wore it every day.
   The hotel was in Sunderland, on top of a high hill.

Page 16 — Using Ellipsis

1. You should have matched these pairs:
   There's a library on Duke Street and Church Street. — there's a library on
   Jason plays tennis on Mondays and Fridays. — he plays tennis on
   I've been to Spain, but my parents haven't. — been to Spain
   Nasreen's puppy, Max, has soft brown fur. — who is called
   She left the class because she wanted to. — leave the class

2. Polly loves baking cakes and biscuits.
   Gordon saw lots of monkeys, but Jade didn't.
   I'm going to stay indoors and read a book.
   (OR) I'm going to stay indoors to read a book.
   Max showed Ian the kitchen and the lounge.

CGP

KS2 English
Targeted Answer Book

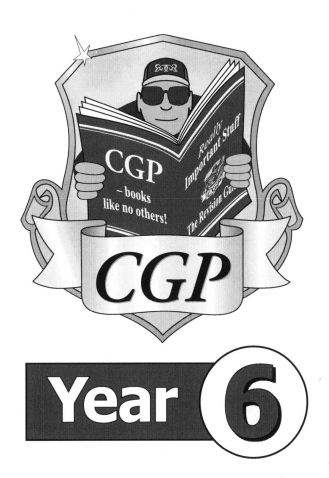

CGP

Year 6

Grammar • Punctuation • Spelling

Contents

Published by CGP

ISBN: 978 1 78294 153 8

Clipart from Corel®
Printed by Elanders Ltd, Newcastle upon Tyne.
Based on the classic CGP style created by Richard Parsons.

Grammar

Section 4 — Tenses

Page 17 — Present Tense and Past Tense

1. You should have ticked these sentences:
   I get up at seven o'clock.
   Leon writes every day.
   We leave at half past one.
   Rewritten sentences:
   I got up at seven o'clock.
   Leon wrote every day.
   We left at half past one.

2. Any sentences which use the words in the boxes and are in the correct tense.
   Examples:
   Present: Jack plays golf.
   Past: Jack played golf.
   Present: We go to the shop.
   Past: We went to the shop.

Page 18 — Present and Past Progressive

1. You should have crossed out these words:
   We (~~are~~ / ~~is~~ / were) (~~plant~~ / planting / ~~plants~~) seeds.
   I (am / ~~was~~ / ~~were~~) (looking / ~~look~~ / ~~looks~~) for my dad.
   He (~~is~~ / ~~were~~ / was) (~~ride~~ / ~~ridden~~ / riding) a horse.

2.

verb	present progressive tense	past progressive tense
to go	Bob **is going** out.	Bob **was going** out.
to win	We **are winning** the race.	We **were winning** the race.
to drive	I **am driving** to France.	I **was driving** to France.
to shut	She **is shutting** a door.	She **was shutting** a door.
to knit	They **are knitting** hats.	They **were knitting** hats.

3. Any sentence which uses at least one 'ing' verb in the past progressive tense.
   Example:
   I was reading a book.

Page 19 — The Perfect Form

1. Any suitable verb in the past perfect form.
   Examples:
   Corrie <u>had moved</u> to Belfast by the time she was six.
   Steve was annoyed because Simon <u>had watched</u> the film already.
   Ruby <u>had given</u> me her old guitar before she bought a new one.
   I <u>had delivered</u> my gran's letters in time for dinner.

2. I have been to a welcome day at my new school. I have put my name down for the netball team, and Jon has joined the art club. We have spoken to our new teacher.

Section 5 — Sentence Structure

Pages 20 and 21 — Subject and Object

1. In the sentences below, the subject is in **bold** and the object is underlined.
   The fox crosses <u>the road</u>.
   Hannah speaks to <u>Samuel</u> calmly.
   The cat chases <u>the squirrel</u>.
   Mairi forgot <u>her sunglasses</u> again.
   Uncle Joe bought <u>a sandwich</u>.
   The bear hugged <u>the tree</u>.
   Yesterday **Ian** read <u>the newspaper</u>.
   The gardener carried <u>the plant pots</u>.

2. You should have labelled the words like this:
   sings — verb   pop songs — object
   The baker — subject   the egg — object
   The grocer — subject   shouted — verb
   The swimmer — subject   the children — object
   met — verb   Mr Potter — object
   Kathryn — subject   a dress — object

3. Each sentence should have been completed with a sensible suggestion, e.g.
   Stephen wrote a newspaper article.
   Sian threw **a ball** across the field.
   The teacher shouted at **the pupil**.
   Grandma made a cheesecake.
   Mrs Huckton broke **her arm**.
   The monkey climbed the tree.

4. Rob <u>drove</u> to the airport. (verb)
   A group of girls <u>ate</u> the ice cream. (verb)
   <u>A bird</u> built a nest in the apple tree. (subject)
   Francesca opened <u>the door</u> nervously. (object)
   <u>Mia</u> doesn't like Sam any more. (subject)

Pages 22 to 24 — Passive and Active Voice

1. The Queen wears a crown. A
   The cleaner scrubbed the floor. A
   The room was tidied by Tim. P
   The balloon was filled with air. P
   Martha tried to catch it. A
   Brian bought a new hat. A
   Nick was pushed by Cameron. P
   The chicken crossed the road. A
   The leaf was blown in the wind. P
   Amy wore a red dress. A
   The speech was made by Tony. P
   My dad was awarded a medal. P

2. The letter was signed by David.
   The sofa was delivered by the men.
   Antonio was hit with a pillow.

3. The sentences should have been rewritten as follows:
   Eleanor was hugged by Auntie Pam.
   Fiona was found in the garden by Paul.
   Ruby and Olivia were picked up by Lizzie.
   The dog was shouted at by the postman.

4. You should have underlined these sentences:
   The first match was won by Lonsdale Lions.
   The Lions were defeated by the Tigers in the second game.
   During the party, the trophy was stolen by a magpie.
   The trophy was returned to the Tigers by PC Harley.
   The sentences should have been rewritten as follows:
   Lonsdale Lions won the first match.
   The Tigers defeated the Lions in the second game.
   During the party, a magpie stole the trophy.
   PC Harley returned the trophy to the Tigers.

5. You should have labelled the words like this:
   <u>Toby</u> was given the letter. — P, subject
   <u>The ball</u> was thrown. — P, subject
   <u>The dog</u> sniffed the acorns. — A, subject
   Pete fixed <u>the window</u>. — A, object
   <u>The cake</u> was eaten by Jo. — P, subject

6. The visitors were welcomed.
   The dog was chased down the road.
   Fizzy drinks were banned at school.

Section 6 — Writing Style

Pages 25 to 27 — Formal and Informal Writing

1. You can't come with us. — I
   You cannot accompany us. — F
   That is unacceptable, Mother. — F
   That's not OK, Mum. — I
   Stephen's got some new wheels. — I
   Stephen has bought a new car. — F
   We really must hurry. — F
   Come on, we'll be late. — I
   Pop along to reception first. — I
   Please report to reception. — F
   I need to find some money. — F
   I need to grab some cash. — I

2. You should have underlined these words:
   chuffed
   stuff
   ta
   corker
   Blimey
   nattered
   Grab
   way
   shattered
   gadding

3. You should have matched these pairs:
   He's coming over later. — He is coming over later.
   Did they have any cash? — Had they any money?
   That's not fair, is it? — Do you think that is fair?

4. Do you wish to dance? — F
   She should've taken an umbrella. — I
   We're meeting them at the park, aren't we? — I
   Mrs Hudson received a present from her friend. — F
   If I were to move abroad, I would live in Spain. — F
   Examples of corrected sentences:
   She should have taken an umbrella.
   Are we meeting them at the park?

5. Across: 1: disappointed
          2: marry
          3: children
          4: relax
   Down: 1: stole
          2: mother
          3: tired
          4: dirty

6. unacceptable
   wonderful
   think
   hoping
   simple
   complaining

Pages 28 and 29 — Writing for Your Audience

1. A letter of complaint to a company. — formal writing
   A postcard to your sister. — informal writing
   A report on rainforests. — formal writing
   An essay about ancient Egypt. — formal writing
   A note for your friend. — informal writing
   A text message to your mum. — informal writing

2. A note to the milkman asking for an extra pint of milk. — I
   A letter to the Queen asking her to visit your school. — F
   A letter to your teacher to apologise for being late. — F
   An email to your auntie asking how her cat is. — I
   A school report about the life cycle of a frog. — F
   An email inviting your friends over for dinner. — I

3. You should have ticked these sentences:
   Thanks for coming mate — it was fab.
   I look forward to receiving your reply.
   We found the experiment very interesting.
   You've nicked my footy boots, haven't you?

4. Example sentences:
   I can't believe you didn't make it.
   Your food is not of a good standard.
   Are you going to ban homework?
   Can you pick me up from school at 4?
   Many children had to clean chimneys.

Grammar

**Pages 30 to 32 — Standard and Non-Standard English**

1. I've asked Paul to speak to ___ farmers. — those
   Penny hasn't heard back from ___ yet. — them
   How did ___ potatoes get there? — those
   Kathy will pick ___ up from the station. — them

2. Nobody can do nothing to stop the floods. — 2
   I haven't got no time to do my homework. — 2
   Joseph couldn't find anywhere to stay. — 1
   Maria doesn't want nobody to leave. — 2

3. You should have matched these pairs:
   You should of gone too. — You should have gone too.
   He could of helped. — He could have helped.
   I might of put it away. — I might have put it away.

4. Grandma (saw / ~~seen~~) the picture that Josh had (~~did~~ / done).
   The sisters (saw / ~~seen~~) a ballet which (~~come~~ / came) to their local theatre.
   Hattie (~~done~~ / did) lots of work, but then she (~~gone~~ / went) home.
   Hassan and Ian have (seen / ~~saw~~) the person who (did / ~~done~~) it.
   Sian and Phil have (come / ~~came~~) to visit, but they have (gone / ~~went~~) out.

5. Charlotte and ___ went for a walk. — I
   Rob shouted at Annabel and ___ . — me
   Alice and ___ were late for dinner. — I
   ___ ran to collect the parcels. — I
   The teacher said it was up to ___ . — me

6. Example sentences:
   He isn't coming on holiday with us.
   I am not impressed with this weather.
   Stefan hasn't seen the film yet.
   I haven't found the lost rabbit.

7. <u>goes</u> — go
   <u>play</u> — plays
   <u>is</u> — are
   <u>was</u> — were
   <u>have</u> — has
   <u>has</u> — have

8. You should have matched these pairs:
   Them robbers stole my bag! — Those robbers stole my bag!
   I don't wanna go. — I don't want to go.
   Ain't you helping? — Aren't you helping?
   We're not bothering no one. — We're not bothering anyone.

9. I think my leg is broken.
   Have you found those geese?
   It wasn't my fault!
   We have been walking for hours. / We were walking for hours.
   The puppy licked Jake and me.
   I haven't done anything.

Punctuation

Punctuation

Section 1 — Sentence Punctuation

Page 2 — Capital Letters and Full Stops

1. The train to Manchester takes two hours.
   Mr Jones married Miss Newton on 1st July.
   I have a cat. It's called Meg.

2. Tomorrow is Mr Frimley's birthday. Mr Frimley is our teacher. We have planned a surprise party for him at lunchtime. Everyone is bringing in something different for us to eat. Will is making a cake and I am bringing party hats and streamers. I hope the party is a success. It took ages to organise.

Page 3 — Question Marks and Exclamation Marks

1. Those lights look amazing!
   Do you want me to help you?
   I enjoy going out for dinner.
   I don't want to go, but...

2. Any sentence which uses the words and punctuation marks correctly.
   Examples:
   Can **Jimmy** do **magic tricks?**
   I would like fly to the **moon** in a **rocket.**
   There's a gang of **zombies** in your **garden!**
   Are your **neighbours friendly?**

Pages 4 and 5 — Sentence Practice

1. I'd like to buy a new car.
   How far away are we from the beach?
   What have I done to deserve this?
   Tom went to the zoo yesterday.
   Let's try this one next.
   Yes, we won!
   Get out of my sight!
   Did you find them?

2. "Help! Help!" shouted Sam. A police officer appeared.
   "What's the problem, Sir?" he asked.
   "I've been robbed!" cried Sam, pointing at a man who was running up the street.
   The policeman chased after the thief, and everyone was surprised to see what happened next...

3. Have you been before?
   Thank you very much.
   I can't see anything!
   Stop that man!
   Do you want a waffle?
   I like the green one.
   Please pass the gravy.
   Come here, now!

4. Can you help me with my homework?
   Some aliens have landed on the roof!
   When can I have my football back?
   Tell me the truth right now!

5. Any sentences that use the words and punctuation mark correctly.
   Examples:
   I saw a **cloud** hovering over Bobby's head.
   That's not a **crocodile**, it's...
   Did you see the **teacher fly** across the classroom?
   There's a **zebra** in the garden!

Section 2 — Commas

Page 6 — Commas in Lists

1. Yesterday, I went to a theme park with Jordan, Carl, Elijah and David. We went on three roller coasters, a log flume, a Ferris wheel and some bumper cars. At lunchtime, we had cheeseburgers with chips, big cups of fizzy pop and a chocolate bar each. We left with big smiles, full tummies and happy memories.

2. Any list that uses commas correctly.
   Examples:
   My mum bought me a new jumper, a pencil case, a folder and a packet of my favourite chocolate bars.
   Emily's favourite foods are pasta, crisps, carrots and sausages.
   In my bedroom, I have a wardrobe, a chest of drawers, a desk and a really big bed.

Page 7 — Commas to Join Sentences

1. I went to the cinema, for it was my birthday.
   I've got a new bike, so I've started cycling to school.
   I bought a ticket for the raffle, and I won first prize.
   I'll walk through the haunted house, or go on the ghost train.

2. I went on holiday, **and** I had a great time.
   My car was broken, **so** I got the train.
   I baked a cake, **but** it tasted horrible.

Page 8 — Commas After Subordinate Clauses

1. You should have ticked:
   Although he can't dance, my dad is usually quite cool.
   Even when it's the weekend, I like to have breakfast at 7 am.

2. As Ben hates coffee, I've made him a hot chocolate.
   Before you start eating, you should wash your hands.
   Even though it was raining, we still had fun.
   Although it is winter, I'd like to swim in the lake.

Page 9 — Commas After Introductions

1. For ten minutes, Lewis tried to solve the puzzle.
   With a big smile, Richard greeted his exchange partner.
   Every evening, I practise the piano.
   In Ancient Egypt, the rulers were called pharaohs.
   On Monday, I'm playing tennis for the county.

2. Any sensible sentences which use a comma followed by a main clause.
Examples:
Before breakfast, I brushed my teeth.
As quickly as possible, he hid the presents in the wardrobe.
Every Wednesday evening, I go to swimming club.
In a large bowl, mix together the first three ingredients.
At the zoo, I saw giraffes and lions.
For twenty minutes, I stared out of the window.

Pages 10 and 11 — Commas for Extra Information

1. The bun, which had lots of icing, was delicious.
The theme, which was films, was very popular.
Mildred, my cat, is very fierce.

2. Today, on our school trip to the zoo, we had a picnic.
Nick, the youngest boy in our class, brought a selection pack of crisps. The salt and vinegar flavoured crisps, which are always everyone's favourite, went first.
Georgina, my best friend, brought a big box of biscuits.
The custard creams, which are my favourites, were very popular. The digestives, a much more boring kind of biscuit, were also very popular. We did have some fruit, mainly oranges and bananas, as well.

3. The competition, which was very difficult, was won by Mr Smith.
Paris, the capital of France, is home to the Eiffel Tower.
The fire, which continued through the night, destroyed the house.

4. Any acceptable extra information that uses commas correctly.
Examples:
My sister, **who is older than me**, is a professional chess player.
My friends, **Emma and Laura**, always laugh at my singing.
My mum baked apple pie, **my dad's favourite**, and it was delicious.
The dog, **which was very hungry**, ate all of its food straight away.

Pages 12 and 13 — Comma Practice

1. Alan, my boss, has an excellent sense of humour.
Before you go, let me give you your present.
So that you can find your way, I'll lend you a torch.
I would come with you, but I just don't have time.
Shall I wear the tie with spots, stripes or stars?
For now, let's just keep doing it like this.

2. Like a professional, he was very polite. — After an adverbial phrase
Sam was frightened of bats, owls and cats. — Separating items in a list
Mr Cole, my neighbour, is amazing at tennis. — Extra information
As you're here, let's go through this now. — After a subordinate clause

3. My football coach, Mr Cameron, is giving me extra training sessions. He thinks I have potential, but my mum thinks I should concentrate more on my schoolwork. Even though I work really hard at school, she still thinks that football is a distraction. Before practice, she always checks that I have done all of my homework. She checks for messy handwriting, spelling mistakes and wrong answers. If I haven't finished my work, I can't go to practice.

4. The race, the 100 m sprint, took place today.
My bike, which is very old, needs repairing.

5. Any list that uses commas correctly.
Example:
If I were rich, I would buy a new house for my parents, pay somebody to do my homework, buy lots of computer games and hire someone to look after my rabbits.

Section 3 — Brackets and Dashes

Page 14 — Brackets for Extra Information

1. The ship (a cruise liner) left at nine o'clock.
Martin (Victoria's husband) is a professional artist.
The snow (six feet deep) meant we stayed at home.
Alan rushed into the café (the one behind the library).

2. Any suitable information added between the brackets.
Examples:
The school trip (**a weekend of hiking**) was a disaster.
Wendy (**Sophie's new puppy**) liked going for long walks.
The farmers (**who'd had enough**) went on holiday.
Mike's bedroom (**which has green walls**) is pretty small.

Page 15 — Dashes for Extra Information

1. The whole family — even Sam — is going on holiday.
Niall's pig — the pink spotty one — loves having mud-baths.
Our wedding — seven months away — will be on a boat.
The suitcase — bulging and heavy — wouldn't fit in the boot.

2. My dog — a German shepherd — enjoys chasing squirrels.
Keith's cousin — an American — travelled to Scotland.

3. Any suitable information added between the brackets.
Examples:
Dr Katich — **the best doctor in town** — arrived at work.
Susannah's car — **an old banger** — wouldn't start.
Ray made dinner — **pork chops** — in the kitchen.
Tim and Naomi — **my two friends** — started laughing.

Punctuation

1. You should have ticked:
   The house was dark — there were no lights on.
   Helen bought three bags of fruit — the apples looked delicious.
   You should have crossed:
   Pedro needed — to find the exit quickly.
   Everyone was going — to the match last night.

2. You should have left in these dashes:
   Andy searched the room — Nicole was nowhere to be seen.
   I had steak and chips for lunch — the steak was excellent.
   Keith stepped outside — it was a cold, frosty morning.
   There was a loud bang — someone had knocked over the teapot.

3. Any suitable clause added after a dash.
   Examples:
   Richard stopped suddenly — he'd just missed the turning.
   Mike and Simon missed the bus — it had left early.
   The crocodile was hungry — it was time for breakfast.

1. My bad-tempered sister slammed the door.
   The price of a second-class stamp has risen dramatically.
   Kat's long-term partner doesn't like her dog.
   Sugar-free doughnuts just don't taste right.
   Our local restaurant only serves home-made food.

2. You should have circled: research, re-sort, re-counted, recall.

Section 4 — Apostrophes

1. should've
   couldn't
   when's
   she'd
   it'd

2. What are we going to do?
   I must have left it behind.
   She will be here soon.
   How is your sister doing?
   You have made it.
   I have not got a clue.

1. the children's smiles
   the gorillas' faces
   the cherries' stalks
   the lizards' tongues

2. Examples:
   The bear's fur is pink.
   Joe's bobsleigh crashed.
   The aliens' ship is lost.
   The cactus's spikes are sharp.

1. I think **it's** under the table.
   The airline cancelled **its** flight.
   My dog loves **its** bed.
   It's been a total disaster!
   The chick went to find **its** nest.
   It's an earthquake — run!
   I think **it's** stopped snowing.
   Don't worry, **it's** going to be fine.

2. You should have circled the underlined words:
   I've just had my book published — it's all about King Arthur and his knights. I'm sure <u>its</u> going to be a bestseller because it's been liked by everyone who's read it so far. <u>It's</u> cover has a picture of the round table, my name and the title in big gold letters. <u>Its</u> going on sale next week — I can't wait!

3. Any sentences which use 'its' and 'it's' correctly.
   Examples:
   It's so hot today.
   The gnome carried its basket.

1. You should have crossed:
   This hospital' staff all wear uniform.
   My business' new product is out today.
   The lion roared and bared it's sharp teeth.
   Corrected words:
   This **hospital's** staff all wear uniform.
   My **business's** new product is out today.
   The lion roared and bared **its** sharp teeth.

2. You should have added these apostrophes:
   Alison's *and* haven't
   Green's *and* shouldn't
   Grandad's *and* won't
   It's *and* river's

3. Any sentence which correctly uses an apostrophe to show possession and an apostrophe for a missing letter.
   Example:
   Rani's pet crocodile can't swim.

Section 5 — Inverted Commas

1. You should have ticked these sentences:
   "Can you pass me those dirty dishes, please?" asked Harini.
   "This," the scientist told us, "is the most deadly jellyfish of all."

2. You should have added these punctuation marks:
    "I am through to the national finals!" cried the gymnast.
    Erik asked, "How do I say 'good morning' in French?"
    Artem yelled as loud as he could, "I've found the secret tunnel!"
    "I always have a sandwich and an apple for lunch," Beth said.
    The police officer said calmly, "Tell me where the money is."
    Marco put up his hand and asked, "Is the answer seventeen?"
    "You've lost my magazine," she said, "and I only bought it today!"
    "If we don't leave now," said Mum angrily, "we'll miss the plane!"

3. "I don't want to go out because it's too hot," said Grandad.
    "We need honey for this recipe," said Amir, "and we have none."
    "Go and ask Lily," said Paul, "if we have any more ketchup."
    "Lucy is a great artist," said Chloe, "but I'm better at sports."

4. "I play football on Mondays," said Luke, "and on Fridays."
    "I like mint ice cream," said Milly, "and vanilla."
    "Do you know," asked Simon, "where we are?"
    "They're coming," said the captain, "so hide the treasure!"

5. Any sentences which use inverted commas correctly with the words in the boxes.
    Examples:
    "Quick, the parrot is escaping!" shouted Lewis.
    "Do you want to play chess?" asked Alfie.

Section 6 — Colons and Semi-colons

Pages 24 and 25 — Colons

1. You should have left in these colons:
    You need several things for the trip: a rucksack, a clipboard and some paper.
    I've forgotten my house keys: I left in such a rush this morning.
    The fire procedure is simple: sound the alarm, leave calmly and call 999.
    I can't possibly eat this: it's got mushrooms in it.
    I don't think this house is suitable: there's a huge hole in the roof.
    My brother has three jobs: painter, removal man and waiter.
    I am going to build a rocket this weekend: I want to go to space.

2. You should have ticked these sentences:
    Nadine has three best friends: Nina, Cat and Molly.
    I can't wait for tomorrow: we're going to a museum.
    I can speak three languages: French, Italian and Thai.

3. Dad has loads of tools in his shed: saws, spanners and hammers.
    The crew feared Captain Rogers: he had never lost a sword fight.
    Enzo was crying in the kitchen: he had burnt the dinner again.
    I have a short Christmas list: a board game, a jumper and a puppy.
    Sabrina has very unusual pets: two spiders, a snake and a hedgehog.
    Pancakes have three main ingredients: eggs, milk and flour.
    I'm going to wear two pairs of tights today: it's freezing outside.
    I'm expecting three packages: a phone cover, a skirt and some boots.
    Rob doesn't like going outside at night: he's afraid of bats.

4. Our bakery sells lots of things: bread, cakes and pastries.
    I have three favourite insects: ladybirds, crickets and bees.
    I play three sports: tennis, netball and hockey.

5. Any sentence about the picture which uses a colon correctly.
    Example:
    The boy is in trouble: he is covered in paint.

Pages 26 and 27 — Semi-colons

1. I got a new bike; my brother got a car.
    My dad is English; my mum is German.
    I love ballet; my cousin loves tap.

2. You should have ticked these sentences:
    Find a place to hide <u>or</u> you'll be in trouble.
    I couldn't believe it <u>but</u> I had come last.

3. Jonas had Geography, where they were taking samples in the field; History, his favourite by far; and then English with Mr Jeffries.
    The trapeze artists flew through the air, effortlessly and skilfully; the magicians, my favourite, made all sorts of things vanish; and the three fire-breathers were truly breathtaking!
    The flight was late, delayed by three hours; the seats were uncomfortable, especially mine; and the in-flight food was horrid.
    Ice skating is difficult: it hurts when you fall over, which happens a lot; you have to be careful with the blades on your boots; and you have to avoid others on the ice, which can be tricky!

4. Gemma baked a cake: first she mixed all the ingredients together; then she spread the mixture into a baking tin; then she baked it for twenty minutes.

Punctuation

Pages 28 and 29 — Colons and Semi-colons

1. I'm growing herbs: basil, mint and thyme.
   I have two sisters: Ally, who has curly hair, and five-year-old Eva.

2. I ate all my vegetables **:** carrots, peas and broccoli.
   We need to clean the house **:** the Queen is coming.
   London is a capital city **;** Ulverston is a small town.
   We have three ducks **:** Beatrice, Eugene and Nigel.
   Grasshoppers have six legs **;** spiders have eight legs.

3. Kim stayed outside: Gran had come round.
   On Monday I bake; on Tuesday I sew.
   Ali groomed her dog: the pageant was tomorrow.
   Harry is a painter; Yuri is a teacher.
   I can make pasta; I can't make pancakes.
   Nico screamed: the room was on fire!

4. You should have added these punctuation marks:
   Everyone had helped with the show: Mrs Dastur had painted the sets, one for every scene; all the children, even the reception class, had made props; and the mayor had let them use the village hall.
   The explorer told an exciting tale: he had waded across rivers, fighting crocodiles in his path; slept in trees, without a hammock, with the monkeys; and examined all sorts of wonderful insects.

Section 7 — Paragraphs and Layout

Page 30 — Paragraphs

1. Paragraph 1: a, d, f, j
   Paragraph 2: c, h, i, l
   Paragraph 3: g, b, e, k

2. You should have added these paragraph markers:
   "Come over here, Ellie," called Grandad, looking up from his potato planting. // "What is it?" I asked, wading over to him through the mud and bags of freshly picked vegetables. // "I want you to learn how to plant seeds," he told me. // "Fine," I replied. I stood and watched obediently, trying to concentrate on Grandad and ignore the worms wriggling at my feet. // "Now, let's see if you've got my magic touch," he smiled, handing me the bag.

Page 31 — Layout Devices

1. 1: heading
   2: subheading
   3: table
   4: bullet points
   5: box

Page 32 — Writing Lists

1. 1) Mix the dry ingredients together.
   2) Whisk the eggs with the milk.
   3) Add the liquid to the dry ingredients.
   4) Spread the mixture into baking tins.
   5) Bake at 180 °C for twelve minutes.

2. Any list of four items using bullet points correctly.
   Example:
   • play with my brother
   • go to the park
   • visit my grandparents
   • read a comic book

Spelling

Spelling

Section 1 — Prefixes

Pages 2 and 3 — Prefixes — 'trans' 'bi' 'tri' and 'semi'

1. **tri**angle, **bi**lingual OR **tri**lingual, **semi**final, **trans**former

2. **trans**port, **semi**finalists, **trans**mission, **bi**annual, **trans**action, **semi**professional, **semi**circles, **tri**cycles

3. **semicircular, transaction, bicycle, transformation, transportation, transfusion, transformed, tricoloured**

4. My brother needs a **transplant**.
   Punctuation is tricky — especially those **semicolons**.
   I'm going on a **transatlantic** trip to America.
   John was **transfixed** by the stars in the sky.
   I've never flown on a **triplane** OR **biplane** before.

Pages 4 and 5 — Prefixes — 'aero' 'micro' 'tele' 'photo' and 'circum'

1. **teleport, aerodynamic, microchip, microsecond, microwave**

2. **aerospace, telescope, microorganism, televised, circumstances, photocopy, circumnavigate**

3. **television, microphone, aeroplane, photograph, telephone, telescope**

4. e.g.
   aero- **aeroplane, aerospace, aerodynamic**
   micro- **microchip, microsecond, microwave, microorganism, microphone**
   tele- **teleport, telegraph, television, telephone, telescope**
   photo- **photocopy, photocopier, photograph, photographer, photography**
   circum- **circumstance, circumnavigate**

Pages 6 and 7 — Hyphenating Prefixes

1. **re-establish, semi-annual, pre-election, pre-install, co-existence, re-enact**

2. **re-evaluate, co-ordinate, de-ice, re-edit, co-own**
   Lawrence and Ivan **co-own** a property in London.
   The windscreen was frozen over, so we had to **de-ice** it.

3. Ronald didn't **react** well to the bad news.
   The play was on three nights in a row, so Finn had to **re-act** his role.
   Mrs Brown made a nasty **remark** to the postman.
   The teacher had to **re-mark** the tests after noticing a mistake.
   Jackie **resigned** from her role as chief chocolate tester.
   I had to **re-sign** the document because it got wet.
   Jim's wound got infected, so the nurse had to **re-treat** it.
   The soldiers had no option but to **retreat** to their bunker.

4. Tom decided to **re-press** the button to check it was working.
   After school, the children often go to the **recreation** ground.
   The end result was the **re-creation** of a classic film.
   Sandy shouldn't **repress** her emotions when she's feeling sad.

5. Any sentences where hyphenated words have been used correctly. Examples:
   Margaret gave a **semi-intelligent** answer to my question.
   Tom had a rash, so he used some **anti-itch** cream.
   Colin wants to **re-establish** himself as a children's entertainer.

Section 2 — Word Endings and Suffixes

Pages 8 and 9 — Word Endings — the 'shus' sound

1. deli**cious**, overambi**tious**, obno**xious**, infec**tious**, ficti**tious**, mali**cious**, unconten**tious**, viva**cious**.

2. anx**ious**, ungra**cious**, cau**tious**, conscien**tious**, atro**cious**, nox**ious**

3. cons**cious**, preten**tious**, scrump**tious**, ambi**tious**, spa**cious**, lus**cious**.

4. **precious, ambitious, gracious**

5. fero**cious**, supersti**tious**, nutri**tious**, non-infec**tious**, uncons**cious**, deli**cious**, conten**tious**

6. Any sentence where the word is used correctly. Examples:
   The man across the street looked very suspi**cious**.
   After the crash, the driver was only semicons**cious**.
   The decision to ban chocolate is simply atro**cious**.

Pages 10 and 11 — Word Endings — the 'shul' sound

1. **essential, preferential, residential, partial, sacrificial**

2. You should have underlined: **antisotial, presidencial, crutial, fatial**.
   The correct spellings are: antiso**cial**, presiden**tial**, cru**cial**, fa**cial**.

3. confiden**tial**, so**cial**, influen**tial**, artifi**cial**, impar**tial**, unsubstan**tial**.

4. substan**tial**, commer**cial**, ini**tial**, provin**cial**, finan**cial**

5. **social, martial, official**

6. Any sentence where the word is used correctly. Examples:
   The company will not tolerate ra**cial** discrimination.
   Carly has the poten**tial** to be a great runner.
   Our camping trip was spoilt by torren**tial** rain.
   It's always not fair when people get preferen**tial** treatment.

Pages 12 and 13 — Word Endings — 'ant' and 'ent'

1. **apartment, inhabitant, extravagant, permanent**

2. You should have circled: **accidant, hesitent, vacent, relevent**.
   The correct spellings are: accid**ent**, hesit**ant**, vac**ant**, relev**ant**.

3. arrog**ant**, sil**ent**, pres**ent**, leni**ent**, evid**ent**, brilli**ant**, observ**ant**, toler**ant**.

4. argum**ent**, frequ**ent**, expect**ant**, eleg**ant**, obedi**ent**, eleph**ant**, confid**ent**, differ**ent**

5. **talent**, **rodent**, **absent**

6. You should have circled: **comm-**, **independ-**.
Any sentence where the word is used correctly.
Examples:
Bob didn't like his mum's comm**ent** — she said he needs to be more independ**ent**.

Pages 14 and 15 — Word Endings — 'ance', 'ancy' and 'ence', 'ency'

1. You should have ticked: **obedience**, **balance**.
You should have crossed: **patiance**, **tolerence**, **substence**, **resistence**.
The correct spellings are: pati**ence**, toler**ance**, subst**ance**, resist**ance**.

2. differ**ence**, experi**ence**, frequ**ency**, insur**ance**, pregn**ancy**, curr**ency**

3. int**elli**g**ence**, app**earance**, ev**idence**, sc**ience**, hin**drance**, nui**sance**, app**liance**.

4. Any sentence where the word is used correctly.
Examples:
Joseph didn't even have the dec**ency** to say sorry.
Performing on stage gave Luke lots of confid**ence**.
I had blonde hair in my inf**ancy**.
In Mrs Smith's abs**ence**, a supply teacher will take the class.

Pages 16 and 17 — Word Endings — 'able' and 'ible'

1. You should have circled: **debatible**, **possable**, **noticeible**, **justifiible**, **fashionible**.
The correct spellings are: debat**able**, poss**ible**, notice**able**, justifi**able**, fashion**able**.

2. comfort**able**, irrespons**ible**

3. consider**able**, forc**ible**, reason**able**, toler**able**.

4. You should have circled: **terrable**, **understandible**, **edable**.
The correct spellings are: terr**ible**, understand**able**, ed**ible**.

5.

Clue	Word
if you can't see something, it's...	in**visible**
if something doesn't stay the same, it's...	chan**geable**
if something is very cute, it's...	ad**orable**
if a story sounds like it's true, it's...	bel**ievable**
if something is not very nice, it's...	hor**rible**
if something can't happen, it's...	imp**ossible**
if something is likely to happen, it's...	pro**bable**
if something is worth a lot of money, it's...	val**uable**

Pages 18 and 19 — Word Endings — 'ably' and 'ibly'

1. forgiv**ably**, responsi**bly**, incredi**bly**, favourably, justifi**ably**, tolerably, regrettably, irresisti**bly**

2. accept**ably**, visi**bly**, misera**bly**, terri**bly**, applic**ably**.

3. reason**ably**, sensi**bly**, horri**bly**, believ**ably**, ador**ably**, remark**ably**.

4. **comfortably**, **legibly**, **understandably**

5. consider**ably**, impossi**bly**, reli**ably**

6. Any sentence where the word is used correctly.
Examples:
Pamela was notice**ably** shocked by the news.
Tyrone behaved respect**ably** — he was very polite to everyone.
I am possi**bly** going to France on Friday.
This antique recognis**ably** dates back to the eighteenth century.

Pages 20 and 21 — Adding Suffixes to Words Ending in 'fer'

1. You should have underlined: **preferrably**, **offerred**, **differring**, **defered**.
The correct spellings are: **preferably**, **offered**, **differing**, **deferred**.

2. **transferring**, **transferred**, **transference**
suffering, **suffered**, **sufferer**

3.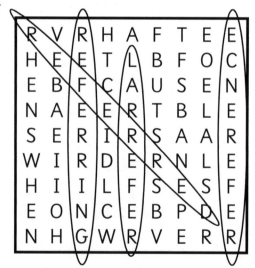

referring, **reference**, **referred**, **referral**

4. **offer**, **infer**, **prefer**
Possible answers include:
offered, **offering**, **offerer**
inferred, **inferring**, **inference**, **inferior**, **inferable**
preferred, **preferring**, **preference**, **preferable**, **preferably**

Spelling

Section 3 — Confusing Words

Pages 22 and 23 — ei and ie Words

1. **wield**, **relieved**, **brief**, **receiver**, **deceive**
2. belie**v**able, fi**e**rce, n**ei**ghbour, r**ei**gn, mischi**e**vous, hyg**ie**ne, conc**ei**ve, achi**e**vable
3. You should have circled: y**eil**d, soc**ei**ty, w**ie**ght, var**ei**ty, rec**ie**pt

   The correct spellings are: y**ie**ld, soc**ie**ty, w**ei**ght, var**ie**ty, rec**ei**pt
4. n**ei**ther, d**ie**sel, perc**ei**ve, **ei**ther, t**ie**r, h**ei**ght
5. **weird**, **seize**, **protein**
6. Any sentence where the word is used correctly.
   Examples:
   The anc**ie**nt Egyptians built the pyramids.
   The th**ie**f stole all the valuables in the house.
   She listened to music to rel**ie**ve the boredom of homework.
   The fr**ei**ght train was travelling across the country.

Pages 24 and 25 — Words with 'ough' in

1. Words with the 'or' sound: **ought**, **thought**, **sought**
   Words with the 'uff' sound: **tough**, **rough**, **enough**
2. **though**, **thorough**, **nought**, **borough**, **brought**
3. **through**, **nought**, **cough**
4. Across clues: 1) **brought** 2) **thoughtful** 3) **fought** 4) **throughout**

   Down clues: 1) **drought** 2) **thought** 3) **plough**
5. Any sentence where the word is used correctly.
   Examples:
   Pigs eat from a **trough**.
   Tony **bought** a sports car.
   To make bread you have to knead **dough**.
   Jenny concentrated **throughout** the lesson.

Pages 26 and 27 — Words with Silent Letters

1. shoul**d**, ex**h**aust, wom**b**, debu**t**, solem**n**, **w**hine, **g**narled, **h**our
2. g**u**ess, **w**reckage, g**h**astly, **w**rinkled, s**c**ene, desi**g**n, beni**g**n, **r**hythm
3. Silent u words: g**u**ess, g**u**itar, g**u**ard
   Silent h words: **r**hinoceros, ve**h**icle, **h**onest
   Silent c words: fas**c**inated, as**c**end, mus**c**le
4. s**c**issors, cas**t**les, **k**night, **w**rist, sal**m**on, hal**f**, buil**d**, mus**c**les, forei**g**n, **k**now
5. autum**n**, r**h**yme, chal**k**, **k**nit, thum**b**
6. Any sentence where the word is used correctly.
   Examples:
   W**h**o is responsible for all this mess?
   The chocolate should be at the back of the cu**p**board.
   That pink handbag isn't very su**b**tle.

Pages 28 and 29 — Confusing Nouns and Verbs

1. Nouns: advi**ce**, licen**ce**, practi**ce**
   Verbs: advi**se**, licen**se**, practi**se**
2. **device**, **prophecy**, **prophesy**, **devise**
3. devi**ce**, devi**se**, advi**ce**, advi**se**, licen**ce**, licen**se**, practi**ce**
4. Any sentence where the word is used correctly.
   Examples:
   There's lots of memory available on my handheld **device**.
   We need to **devise** a plan to get rid of these mice.
   I forgot to do my piano **practice** last week.
   When are we going to **practise** our dance routine?
   I asked my mum for **advice** about what to do.
   Please can you **advise** me of your new address.

Pages 30 to 32 — Homophones

1. write   bridal
    altar ascent
2. **effects**, **complimentary**, **Whose**, **draught**, **assistants**, **lesson**
3. **peek**, **sent**, **medal**, **meddle**, **peak**, **scent**
4. You should have written the words: **prophet**, **allowed**, **missed**, **knot**, **passed**, **whether**, **groan**, **plain**, **cereal**
   The hidden message is **homophone.**
5. You should have made: **farther**, **descent**, **dissent**, **father**
   The homophones are **farther** / **father** and **descent** / **dissent**.
6. Any sentence where the word is used correctly.
   Examples:
   Who's going in **whose** car?
   The **boy** swam out to the **buoy**.
   The **principal** outlined his main **principles**.
   In the **past** I would easily have **passed** this test.

Do not connect directly to mains electricity

ISBN 978 1 78294 153 8

9 781782 941538

E6SA21   £2.00
              (Retail Price)

www.cgpbooks.co.uk